ENGLISH COUNTRY PUBS

JOHN CURTIS
Text by Richard Ashby

SALMON

THE BARLEY MOW

INTRODUCTION

While the Norman invaders drank wine they found that there was already a well-established tradition of beer drinking in these islands and they lost little time in licensing ale-houses and thus gaining a useful source of revenue. So the village pub has been an important part of the landscape in England for many centuries now, serving a local community, and is the true descendant of the medieval ale-house. Inns, in contrast, began by meeting the needs of travellers and often were monastic in origin. Today this distinction has gone and they each have their own unique character. The English pub is an institution, there is nothing quite like it elsewhere in the world, and the village pub is as much a centre of the village as the church. They are usually near each other and indeed often linked, both by the shared clientele (bell ringers and sextons especially having prodigious thirsts) and, usually in the imagination or legend, by a secret tunnel running between the two (though why this should be necessary in a country where the Church has never officially tried to ban drinking is not explained)! Generally the village pub continues to flourish. As village amenities, the shop and the post office, are closed, and people increasingly commute to the nearest town to work or to shop, it is the pub which helps keep the community alive and brings together both those who live in the village and those who are looking for the charm and character possessed by the best English pubs.

The Barley Mow *Clifton Hampden, Oxfordshire*

ROYAL OAK INN

Winsford, Somerset

This thatched village pub, originally a farmhouse and a dairy dating from the 12th century, developed into an inn serving the packhorses and carts which carried the wool produced locally on the West Somerset hills to the markets in Exeter and Tiverton. In its well-preserved village it is everyone's idea of what an English country pub should be.

THE BLACK LION

High Roding, Essex

Situated on the road between Great Dunmow and Chipping Ongar, formerly two important agricultural centres, though not very far from London, this is a 14th century coaching inn, black and white half timbered outside and with low ceiling, black beamed bars inside.

THE BLACK LION
BLACK LION
FINE ALES
TEA
COFFEE
BLACK LION
BANK HOLIDAY
MONDAY:
FOOD SERVED
12-2pm
7-9pm
RIDLEYS
FOOD
Lunch
12 – 2
EVENING
7 – 9
RIDLEYS

THE LAUREL
INN

THE LAUREL INN

Robin Hood's Bay, North Yorkshire

Sometimes known as 'The Clovelly of the North', this red-roofed fishing village scrambles down the cliff to its harbour through a maze of narrow, stepped and cobbled streets and alleys. Tucked away is the little Laurel Inn, clinging to the cliff face, with a bar carved out of rock.

THE RED LION

Weobley, Herefordshire

Weobley is one of north Herefordshire's lovely 'black-and-white' villages. It is full of half timbered houses and the Red Lion, a former coaching inn, dates back to the 14th century. At the rear is a 'cruck' framed cottage, reputed to be the oldest in England.

THE BAT AND BALL

Hambledon, Hampshire

Hambledon Cricket Club was founded around 1750 and the nearby pub was the clubhouse. For a time it was the centre of English cricket and here many of the rules that govern the game today were instituted. Opposite the pub is a granite obelisk on which are carved two cricket bats, a ball and two (not three) stumps.

OLD ALBION

Crantock, Cornwall

The inn is named after a schooner which was built at the shipyard on the Gannel estuary a mile or so away. It is some four hundred years old. At one time smuggling was rife in the area and under a stone by the fireplace in the lounge is access to a smugglers' hole which passes in secret under the village.

Old Albion
Fine
ALES
WINES
Spirits

THE COACH AND HORSES

Wicken Bonhunt, Essex

Although the church owned a 'brew house' in the village at the beginning of the 19th century there was no real 'pub' until this attractive building became one some fifty years later. The pub sign depicts a horse-drawn coach, in which the passengers' faces are those of past and present villagers.

PILCHARD INN

Burgh Island, Devon

The name commemorates the fishing industry and the fish which was the mainstay of those who lived and worked here over the centuries. Originally a cottage, the pub dates back to the 14th century. Burgh Island is only accessible on foot at low tide, whilst at other times a unique 'sea tractor' conveys visitors across the water to the pub and the exclusive Art Deco hotel nearby.

THE FOUR HORSESHOES

Thornham Magna, Suffolk

As you would expect Thornham Magna is the larger of the two Thornham villages in Suffolk, midway between Diss and Stowmarket. This pretty picture-postcard thatched pub was built in 1150 and has within it an ancient well.

THE RED LION

Avebury, Wiltshire

The pub sits in the centre of the Neolithic stone circle, surrounded by the huge stones an earthworks. Within the foundations of the pub is said to be the 'Altar Stone', the exact centre the circle and the focus for its builders' rituals.

THE RED LION

BLACK BULL
BLACK BULL
GREAT FOOD
COSTA
Accommodation

BLACK BULL

Haworth, West Yorkshire

This Yorkshire town is famous as the home of he Brontë sisters, Anne, Charlotte and Emily, who lived at the vicarage with their father, Patrick, the perpetual curate of the parish. t is difficult to imagine any of the sisters or their father being patrons of any of the public houses in the town, since Patrick Brontë had founded a local temperance union. However, Branwell, the dissolute brother, was different. Unlike his sisters he was a literary and artistic failure. He was acked by the railway company for which e worked, took to opium and drink and could often be found in The Black Bull, where his chair can still be seen.

THE WENSLEYDALE HEIFER

West Witton, North Yorkshire

Wensleydale is famous for its distinctive cheese and this whitewashed stone pub, a 17th century coaching inn, celebrates its source with its name and its fine sign. West Witton is at the heart of the Yorkshire Dales National Park and a good centre from which to explore the spectacular countryside and its many attractions. The author, James Herriot, was a customer here in his early days as a vet.

SMITH'S ARMS

Godmanstone, Dorset

This is one of the smallest pubs in England and is made of mud and flint. It is said that when King Charles II came this way he asked the blacksmith to serve him a drink. The smith declined, saying he had no licence, on which the King immediately granted him one! The smithy has been a pub ever since.

THE MASONS ARMS

Branscombe, Devon

Originally this was another very smal pub, with just one bar measuring 16 fee square, although by taking over th adjoining cottages the pub has sinc grown rather. It dates back to 1360 an was a Devon cider house selling th produce of the local orchards

The
MASONS
ARMS
Branscombe
HOTEL
YE
TOIL NOT

KIRSTY

THE SHROPPIE FLY

Audlem, Shropshire

A 'fly' was a particularly fast barge. At Audlem, on the Shropshire Union Canal, the mill has been converted into a pub. Its unique feature is the bar made from a narrowboat which has somehow been installed inside.

SUN INN

Dent, Cumbria

The owner of 'The Sun' came to this village with the intention of starting a brewery and selling beer through his pub. Made with local spring water, the beer has proved very popular with both locals and visitors alike.

CAT AND FIDDLE

Hinton Admiral, Hampshire

Though the pub sign bears a picture of a cat and a fiddle it is likely that the origin of the pub name is not the nursery rhyme at all but rather a dedication to Caterine la Fidèle, though who this lady might be is not known. The pub has its origins as a hostel for pilgrims making their way to the priory at Christchurch through the New Forest.

TAN HILL INN

Arkengarthdale, North Yorkshire

At 1732ft above sea level this is the highest pub in England. Sitting astride the Pennine Way on the edge of the Yorkshire Dales National Park, Tan Hill is where Cumbria, North Yorkshire and County Durham meet. This was once a busy area. Coal was being mined here perhaps as early as the Roman period, certainly by the 12th century and an inn is noted here in 1586. The present building dates from the 17th century and there were miners' cottages nearby until the early part of the 20th century. Now it is entirely isolated and must be a very welcome sight indeed to hungry and thirsty walkers tramping the long distance footpaths. It is also an attractive tourist destination in its own right and is the centre of a sheep fair, inaugurated in 1851, and held every year at the end of May.

THE BOAT INN
Free House
The Boat Inn
FREE HOUSE
INDIAN
CHIEF
01604
862428

THE BOAT INN

Stoke Bruerne, Northamptonshire

This canal-side village is a major canal centre on the Grand Union Canal and the home of the National Waterways Museum. The limestone thatched pub lies next to the locks and not far from the Blisworth canal tunnel which is said to be haunted.

THE CASTLE INN

Edgehill, Warwickshire

This Gothick folly was built in 1742 to commemorate the hundredth anniversary of the battle of Edgehill, the first military engagement between the forces of Charles I and those of Parliament in the Civil War. The tower is a replica of Guy's Tower at Warwick Castle. It is sited on the edge of the hill some seven hundred feet above sea level, and there are commanding views of the site of the battlefield.

THE OLD BULL

Inkberrow, Worcestershire

The characters in *'The Archers'*, the long-running radio series, have often enjoyed a quiet pint here, for this pub is the model for 'The Bull' at Ambridge. Charles I and Shakespeare are both also said to have stayed here.

DRUNKEN DUCK INN

Hawkshead, Cumbria

The landlady, finding her ducks lying in the road, started to pluck them, ready for the pot. Noticing signs of life she realised that they had been drinking from a ditch into which a barrel was leaking! Hence the pub name.

DRUNKEN DUCK
INN

BLACK HORSE

Pluckley, Kent

The village is said to be the most haunted
n the country with at least ten ghosts. The
ub has one of its own, Jessie Brooks, who
was killed by a ball in the skittle alley when
he pub was in previous premises and who
noved with the pub to its new home!

THE TROUT

Godstow, Oxfordshire

The Trout originated as the guest house for Godstow Nunnery. It dates from 1133 and was later enlarged incorporating stones from the nunnery after that was sacked in the Civil War. The pub often features in the *Inspector Morse* books and the television films.

TOWER BANK ARMS

Sawrey, Cumbria

Behind the pub is 'Hill Top', the home of Beatrix Potter, author and illustrator of the *Peter Rabbit* books. The 17th century Tower Bank Arms appears in a picture in *Jemima Puddleduck* with a butcher's cart drawn up outside. Both house and pub are now owned by The National Trust. The clock in the gable of the porch is quite unusual.

JAMAICA INN

Bolventor, Cornwall

Bodmin Moor is a lonely and windswept place at the best of times, and such places as this posting house, where horses could be changed and refreshment taken, must have been most welcome to the traveller through Cornwall. It came to fame through the 1936 novel by Daphne du Maurier but was notorious long before as a meeting place for smugglers.

SMUGGLERS' BAR

ACCOMMODATION
RESTAURANT
BAR SNACKS
BEER GARDEN
CAR PARK
HARK to BOUNTY
HARK TO BOUNTY

HARK TO BOUNTY

Slaidburn, Lancashire

This ancient pub, in a pretty stone-built village in the middle of the Forest of Bowland, dates from the 13th century. It was originally called 'The Dog' and its present title refers to 'Bounty', a hound. It is said that the local Squire, who was also the Rector and Master of the Hounds, was drinking in the pub one day after the hunt and, recognising the noise from his favourite hound above the rest of the pack outside, shouted 'Hark to Bounty'. Outside the pub is a staircase leading to a first floor room which for centuries served as the court house for this remote area. It was last used for such purposes as late as 1937 and still contains the jury box and judge's bench.

PANDORA INN

Mylor Bridge, Cornwall

You can sail your yacht and moor it to the pontoons right outside this ancient thatched pub. Situated on one of the many inlets which make up the Carrick Roads, Falmouth's natural harbour, it has a long association with the sea. The 'Pandora' was the ship sent to Tahiti to capture the mutineers from the 'Bounty'.

ALTISIDORA

Bishop Burton, East Yorkshire

Altisidora, owned and trained by Squire Watt of this village, was a very famous racehorse of her day and won the St Leger in 1813. She is commemorated in this pub which faces the village pond and the green on which John Wesley preached beneath an elm tree. A bust of the evangelist, carved from the tree, is in the parish church.

Published in Great Britain by J. Salmon Ltd., Sevenoaks, Kent TN13 1BB. Telephone 01732 452381. Email enquiries@jsalmon.co.uk
Design by John Curtis.
ISBN 1-902842-61-8 Printed in Italy © 2005

Title page photograph: The Falkland Arms, Great Tew *Oxfordshire*.
Front cover photograph: Bewicke Arms, Hallaton *Leicestershire*. Back cover photograph: The White Horse, Chilham *Kent*